Behind The Smiles

Gaylean Maynard

Copyright © 2025 Gaylean Sharon Maynard

ALL RIGHTS RESERVED. NO part of this book may be reproduced or transmitted in any form by any means, electronic or mechanical, including photocopying and recording, or by any information storage and retrieval system, except as may be expressly permitted in writing from the author.

ISBN: 978-1-966968-55-9

Published by:

www.owlpublishers.com
360 S Market St, San Jose, CA 95113,
United States.

Printed in the United States of America

DEDICATION

This book is dedicated to those persons who are willing to go beyond limitations and mediocrity and diligently pursue their predestined purpose on earth. I also dedicate this book in memory of the two most influential persons in my life - my grandmother Evelyn Burrows (1906 - 1989), who instilled godly and moral values in my life, and my precious mother Joanne Cecelia Burrows (1938-2007), who left an indelible imprint upon my life.

FORWARD

The Apostle Paul wrote in 2 Corinthians 12:10,"I take pleasure in infirmities, in reproaches, in needs, in persecutions, in distresses, for Christ's sake. For when I am weak, then I am strong."

"Behind the Smiles" is the riveting life story of Gaylean Maynard, a Bahamian woman of God whose rite-of-passage conveys the message that God will get in the midst of tragedy and cause us to triumph. Maynard's honest and open sharing raises several issues typically faced by island women in marriage, family and domestic-related responsibilities, coupled with the hard press of abuse. What Maynard reveals through strength of character is that seemingly overwhelming odds in this life always turn into overcoming victory in the hands of God. In one of the most interesting parts of the story, Maynard shows how the miracle of God's love and grace embraces us at our most vulnerable moments.

A must read, "Behind the Smiles" is a monumental story that best illuminates 2 Corinthians 4:7:"But we have this treasure in earthen vessels that the excellence of the power may be of God and not of us."

Gaylean Maynard has served as an ordained Intercessory and Preaching Elder at Southside Christian Ministries in Nassau, Bahamas, and has been a sustained example of triumph for all those who serve the Body of Christ. According to her life story, she never stopped smiling. It was her grace gift. Get ready for God to revolutionize your outlook as you read "Behind the Smiles".

Apostle C. Clifford Smith III, CMS, MA, MDiv, PhD Senior Pastor, Southside Christian Ministries

Nassau Bahamas

PREFACE

Beloved, it is never too late to pursue your God-given purpose and destiny. As you read this book, I will take you on a journey that will challenge and motivate you to diligently press beyond stagnation that might have held you in captivity because of life's circumstances. I have had many tests and trials. However, I used them as stepping stones to move forward to my predestined purpose on earth. The plans God has for our lives are good! His thoughts toward us are peace and not evil, to give us an expected end. Nothing happens in our lives by chance. Our lives are God-ordained, and whatever challenge comes our way, Creator God knows about it and is working it out for our good and, most importantly, His purpose.

The devil comes to kill our dreams, steal our purpose and creativity, and destroy our destiny, but Jesus came that we may have life and have it abundantly. The enemy often paints a picture in our mind to cause us to see the challenges of life bigger than they really are. It is only an illusion! We have everything we need on the inside of us our dreams and visions.

"So God created man in His own image; in the image of God He created him; male and female He created them. Then God blessed them, and God said to them, be fruitful, fill the earth and subdue it; have dominion over the animals of the sea, over the birds of the air and over every living thing that moves on the earth." (New King James Version Bible, Genesis 1:27-28) Despite the odds, we have been given a mandate to be fruitful and multiply on the earth. Hence, we should embrace the process of change. I declare you will come forth victorious. The Holy Spirit will give you peace in the midst of every storm you encounter and as you trust Him, He will lead and guide you along life's journey. I declare your life will never be the same, and you will be encouraged to move forward by faith in God.

TABLE OF CONTENT

Introduction 1
Chapter 1: In the Beginning.. 3
Chapter 2: School Days 7
Chapter 3: Courtship and Marriage 9
Chapter 4: Challenging Times 13
Chapter 5: A New Life.. 15
Chapter 6: Testing Times 18
Chapter 7: A Turn-Around 21
Chapter 8: Moving Forward 24
Chapter 9: The Next Move 27
Chapter 10: Perfect Peace 32
Chapter 11: Faith for the Next Move... 37
In Appreciation.. 39
About the Author... 41
About the Book 43

INTRODUCTION

I am sitting at Nassau International Airport, now called Sir Lynden Pindling International Airport, in the Bahamas, waiting for my American Airlines flight to Orlando, Florida, to attend a leadership conference. As I wait for my flight to depart, I am in deep thought. I look up and make eye contact with a man I have not seen in sixteen years. Beside him is a woman, whom I recognize as his wife from behind; I have not seen her in sixteen years either. I walk over to the couple, and we greet each other, excited to reconnect after so many years. The woman and I start talking, and I mention that I saw her in the newspaper sharing a story about how, after many years, she transitioned from one career to a new one. She talks about the challenges she faced during her career transition. I listen carefully and feel inspired because I am about to leave my twenty-year career. This encounter feels like divine timing!

The lady's husband interrupts us to sell me a book he wrote. As he offers to sell it, my spirit leaps inside. Three years earlier, I had a strong feeling in my heart to write a book. The couple's flight is announced, and I am left alone with my thoughts. My flight is called, and I start my walk to the plane, all the while thanking God for the divine encounter at the airport. On that day, destiny unfolded for me. The plane takes off, and in my diary, I begin to write my story, the book you are holding in your hands....

BEHIND THE SMILES

CHAPTER 1: IN THE BEGINNING

The Formative Years

The Extended Family

I was born on January 28, 1959, to the late John Brown and the late Joanna Burrows in the tranquil settlement of Bannerman Town on the Island of Eleuthera in the Bahamas. My parents met in the country's capital, Nassau, on the Island of New Providence. My mom had left her rural island life to seek employment in the "city". Soon after moving to Nassau, my mom became involved with my dad and got pregnant with me. Around the time she got pregnant, she learned my dad was courting another woman who later became his wife. I was told my mom was so hurt by my dad's actions that she tried to abort me. However, God had plans for my life. She later told me my dad was the only man she ever loved. However, despite her hurt, she moved on with her life.

In those days, my grandmother was a midwife, so Mom returned to Bannerman Town until the time of my arrival. Once I was born, she took me back to Nassau for a short time to live with her. At this time, my dad had a chance to visit me and took me to see his siblings. They fell in love with me. My dad tried to convince my mom to give me away to one of his sisters, but Mom did not agree with his plans.

About two years after giving birth to me, Mom got involved with another man and became pregnant with my brother Rickey. Grandmother was the midwife for the delivery of my brother also. As time went by, Mom decided to take Rickey and me back to Eleuthera to live with our grandmother because she did not have anyone to attend to us while she worked. Mom had two more daughters, Georgan and Leila. Mom kept our sisters with her in Nassau and continued to work so she could send money for Rickey and me. I missed my mom, but yet, I smile.

The Formative Years

Our grandmother, Evelyn Burrows, was a precious soul. She was a godly woman who greatly feared the Lord. She got up very early to pray and made sure we were up to pray with her. Mother, as we called her, called out the names of all her children and grandchildren as well as other family and friends when she prayed. She was faithful to God and committed to her church and family. She was a matriarch in the family and the community. We were raised in a God-fearing, strict environment with good Christian values. Mother loved people from all walks of life. As a midwife, she delivered many babies on the island and cared for the mothers and babies for many weeks after birth. Mother was also a farmer, and Rickey and I were her little helpers. We had to go with her every time she went to the farm, and if we rebelled, she would whip us.

We learned quickly to pay close attention to everything Mother said because we did not want to feel her wrath. We had to walk for miles to the farm and work extremely hard in addition to going to school. We rested only when we ate! Rickey was rebellious many times, and each time, he got whipped. I was not woman enough to utter a word against Mother's discipline. I knew if I did, I would receive greater discipline because I was the older one. Mother taught me to cook, clean, and care for people. She wanted me to be perfect at everything I did. I did not realize it at the time, but she was grooming me for the future. Despite her strong disciplinarian actions, she loved us dearly. It seemed harsh at times, but I loved my grandmother and looked on those days with a smile.

The Extended Family

During the summer, Rickey and I visited our sisters and other family members in Nassau. This was an exciting time for us because Nassau was the city with more activities for children. Mom was a God-fearing woman; she made sure we attended Sunday school and other religious activities regularly. We also went to the movie theatres, on shopping sprees, and attended many family functions. Shopping sprees were my favorite! My mom's sisters, Aunt Ruth and Aunt Eulita made sure we enjoyed our summer vacations by giving us the best of everything. They were so precious and special to us. My life was impacted by how they interacted with each other and their friends. In addition, they faithfully cared for their families with integrity. Their moral lives left a lasting impression on my life. The times I spent in Nassau did not go by without me spending special moments with my dad's sisters too. I also met some of my uncles and cousins on my dad's side. They were happy to have me around them. I felt so loved!

Those summers in Nassau with Mom were bittersweet times. My sisters and I did not bond the way we should have. They had special friends in their lives with whom they spent most of their time. I always felt left out, but yet I was always smiling. I was afraid to tell my mom how I was feeling. I also did not know how to express those feelings to my sisters. By this time, rejection was a familiar foe, given that I was rejected in the womb when my mom tried to abort me because of the rejection from my dad. My sisters seemed to be very happy moving along with their lives while I was crying on the inside for their attention. However, in all of this, God still had a plan for my life.

One summer, I met my paternal grandfather while I was visiting one of my aunts. He fell in love with me at first sight. He lived on the Island of Farmers Cay, Exuma, in the Bahamas and was in Nassau because of illness. The short time I spent with him was very interactive. Granddad wanted to know all about me, and he assured me of my acceptance into the family. He died of cancer not very long after we met. I mourned his passing deeply. Even though I met and spent time with my dad's family, I did not have much contact with Dad. Despite this fact, I continued to love him unconditionally. I visited him on numerous occasions at his workplace, just to spend time with him. I could not see him at his home because I was never invited and felt I would not be accepted there.

Christmas was a special time when my mom and her sisters joined Mother, Rickey and me in Bannerman Town, Eleuthera. I looked forward to these visits with expectancy knowing they were coming with many gifts and baked sweets. Aunt Ruth was an excellent cook and took charge of family gatherings with her iron will. The older women would spend hours talking about the old days and visiting with family and friends in the community.

I was content and happy with Mother, but I wanted to be with my mom, sisters and the rest of my family. However, despite my uncontrollable tears, she did not concede to my request. I was so disappointed. I got over it quickly, though, and moved on.

I believe God was ordering my steps all along. The Creator God holds our future in His hands, even when we are out of fellowship with Him. My friend, trust God with your future. You are not here by chance. You were always in the mind of God regardless of how you came into the world. The Sovereign God fearfully and wonderfully made you. Knowing this helps me smile amid every challenge.

As time went by, Mother could not handle Rickey's behavior. In the summer of 1973, she packed up Rickey's belongings and took him to Nassau to Mom.

I was not happy with him leaving because he was the only sibling there with me. Rickey was missed by all of his childhood friends, especially Eddie. In November 1973, Mother received sad news from Mom that Rickey had been knocked down while roller-skating in the street and died instantly. The news was heartbreaking for us, especially Mother. Rickey had just left Eleuthera less than six months prior.

Mom's reaction to the tragedy was to go into shock. She did not shed a tear from the day the accident occurred while making the funeral arrangements. Rickey was only 12 years old. Mom had lost her only son, and this was devastating. Throngs of people came by to give their condolences. I was 14 years of age and did not really understand the dynamics of death. However, based on everyone's reactions, I knew Rickey would never be with me again. It was hard to smile during this difficult time for the family.

CHAPTER 2: SCHOOL DAYS

I began school at the Bannerman Town all-age school. Mr. Eugene Gibson was my first principal. He was a strong disciplinarian and taught the entire school. In those days, there was no division of classes and every student, regardless of age, was in the same classroom. This was a lot of fun! My special friends were Rhoda McKenzie, Joy Finley and Harry Gibson. We did things that only children would do.

Harry gave me a Cracker Jack ring and told me he was in love with me. I showed it to the entire school. I was only ten years old. What did we know about love at such an age? We were enjoying the sweet innocence of youth. Mother never heard about this, or else I would have gotten a whipping. When Mr. Gibson and his family left Eleuthera and returned to Nassau, Father Thaddeus Pratt, and his wife Florence became our teachers. They were also very strict disciplinarians and very passionate about seeing we excel academically so we could have a better future. I recall going to school with my hair not braided, and Father Pratt made me go home and have my hair braided. I was angry but could not show it, or else my teacher at school and my grandmother at home would have whipped me. After the Pratts, for a brief time, I was under the tutelage of Mr. Goliath Burrows and his wife Joyce.

In September 1973, I walked through the doors of Preston H. Albury High School in Rock Sound, Eleuthera. This school was some 30 miles from where I lived. I, along with other students, were bused to school. It was an interesting and exciting time for me. This was an opportunity to interact with students from other towns. We conversed about what was happening in school, as well as happenings in our respective towns, lives and families. I made some loyal friends in high school. The most memorable aspect of my school years was how the boys treated the girls with the utmost respect. They protected us in the only way they knew how.

The principal at that time was Mr. Everette Cartwright, a native of Long Island, Bahamas. He was another strong disciplinarian from the "old school," and he hardly ever smile. I had many favorite teachers, such as Laurie Gibson, Rosalie Gibson, Alsth Deleveaux, and Abdul Khalfani. They influenced my life with their passion to see their students excel in everything they were taught. They were always pleasant and showed tremendous patience toward the students.

In 1976, I was given a history assignment for homework. I hated this subject with a passion and decided I would rebel and not do the assignment. The next day when asked why I did not complete the assignment, I bluntly replied, "I just did not feel like doing it." I did not wait to see what would be the consequences of my actions. I packed up all my books, walked out of the classroom, and never returned. When I walked out of Preston H. Albury High School that day, I thought I was hurting the teacher. I was so young and foolish, and I thought I was a woman, ready to face the world. Despite this, I concur with the old adage, "School days are the best days of your life".

Surprisingly, Mother did not punish me for walking out of school. I believe it was because I was already talking to a young man. During my time at high school, I met a young man who was managing an auto parts store and he showed much interest in me. He came by to introduce himself to my grandmother, and she fell in love with him at first sight. In those days, getting married to a "good man" was very important. Having a good job and a home was all that was required to be considered a "good man". In addition, marriage at an early age was expected and encouraged. At the time, leaving school seemed to have no real impact on my life. However, there are always consequences for the wrong choices we make in life! Sometimes, these consequences do not affect our lives until later in life. Until then, you smile because you have no idea what is ahead.

CHAPTER 3: COURTSHIP AND MARRIAGE

Once I left school, the young man from the auto parts store, Nod, showed an even greater interest in me. We lived thirty miles apart, but that did not prevent him from traveling back and forth to spend time with me. Eventually, Nod expressed his interest in marrying me. When he told Mother, she was excited. In those days, a man from another town was considered an eligible candidate for marriage. In addition, he managed the auto parts store, so he was thought to be a really good man.

When we met, I was only sixteen, and he was twenty-four years old. I really did not understand what I was getting into. I was not taught how to prepare myself for a mate. The Bible states that the older women were to teach the younger ones, but I did not get this. Nod, and I never discussed our dreams and visions to decide if we were compatible with each other in a lifelong relationship. Both of us were ignorant of the fact that we needed counseling before making major decisions about our future as a couple.

I learned the hard way that any potential relationship toward marriage commitment must be built on a foundation of friendship. Friendship uncovers hidden things about each other that need to be discovered and dealt with before commitment to marriage. When life challenges come your way, the friendship will keep the relationship intact. So many marriages fail because couples fall in love without first building a friendship. Friendship reveals who you really are as a person. It also reveals your strengths and shortcomings. Those need to be revealed before marriage so that the two individuals can make an informed decision.

I went through many changes during our courtship. At times, I wanted to tell Nod that we should just call it quits, but I was afraid Mother would be upset with me. She looked up to Nod as a God-sent mate for me. However, he was not familiar with being in a healthy relationship. I felt alone so many times when we were together. Mother saw no wrong in Nod, and in her opinion, which was a common opinion in that era, once a young man came to the home of a young lady, he was good enough for marriage. I did not do a background check on Nod's family history. This information should play a vital role in determining whether you want to make a lifelong commitment to a person. Generational curses can wreak havoc in a marriage if both couples do not investigate each other's family backgrounds. This was my misfortune.

A couple of months before Nod proposed to marry me, I knew he was not the man with whom God ordained for me to spend the rest of my life. I remember one Sunday morning I told my grandmother that I did not think Nod was for me and I did not want to marry him. My grandmother's reply was, "You just don't want a decent man". Even though I was young, I knew enough to know that things were just not comfortable in my spirit. Mother thought he was decent because he had a home, a car, and a job, and nothing else mattered. Although Mother loved me, this was all she knew. After our conversation, I ran away to the beach and cried uncontrollably. I needed my grandmother to understand what I was trying to tell her. I felt hurt and unloved and wanted desperately to talk to someone who would hear my heart cry, but there was no one. I was very immature and did not understand fully what I was getting into. However, I knew Nod was not the person I wanted to be with for the rest of my life. Nonetheless, we got married on December 24, 1977, and it was a huge event. My family from both sides came from Nassau to Eleuthera for the celebration. My father also came, and I was so excited that he had consented to be my father's giver. I loved my father although he did not play much of a father's role in my life. People also came from all over the island of Eleuthera to help Nod, and I celebrate our vows. The wedding ceremony and reception were beautiful! This was a life-changing event in my life.

When all the fun and excitement was over, we had our honeymoon, and then reality hit. Two weeks into our marriage, Nod began to abuse me physically. I was so devastated that I packed all my belongings and went back to my grandmother. Mother did not welcome me back. Because, in her eyes, Nod could do no wrong. My mom and other family members were aware of the treatment I was receiving; however, no one came to my rescue. I was left alone to battle things out on my own. I decided it was in my best interest to stay in the marriage. I had no way of escaping this horrifying experience.

Not long after our marriage, Nod lost his job at the auto parts store, and I was pregnant with our first child. Nod continued to abuse me physically, even though I was with a child. During those times, I was terrified. I tried to talk with Mom about the abuse, but she did not believe me. She told me I was the one causing the fights. My grandmother loved Nod so dearly that she did not entertain what I had to say. Nod, and I tried to work things out, but he was always swayed by other people's opinions.

Nod came from an abusive environment. His stepfather physically abused his mother, so he thought it was ok to do the same. Many marriages break apart because of deep-rooted generational curses passed down from one generation to the next. We never received professional or pastoral counseling. In retrospect, I believe God was with me even though I did not have a relationship with Him. His hands were upon me for purpose and destiny.

Our oldest daughter was born on March 25, 1979. This was a time of great celebration for Mom and us. This was the arrival of my first child and her first grandchild. By this time, Nod had another job in another island. Those days were difficult for me because I needed Nod to help me with our daughter. Two years later, our second daughter was born on April 14, 1981. The fights did not cease, in fact, they continued more intensely. He fought me in front of our children, and they were both traumatized. I realize now that you cannot give what you never received. Nod never received love from his father. Therefore, he did not know how to love me. I thought that sex was love, so I thought he was loving me. I had no one to groom me for marriage.

I suffered ten years of physical abuse with no support from my family. I cried in secret almost every day because I never wanted the children to see my tears. I started to drink alcohol to suppress my unhappiness. One night in December 1987, we had a terrible fight. I decided that was the last abuse I was going to endure. I left home that night for good and only returned the next day for my clothes. He did not allow me to take the girls; he used this as a strategy for me to return. I left and never returned.

Many couples are joined together for the wrong reason and as a result, the marriages end in divorce. God's ideal plan for marriage is one man for one woman for a lifetime. The lust of the eyes and flesh will cause men and women to end up in relationships not ordained by God. The scripture declares, "But seek first the kingdom of God and his righteousness and all these things shall be added unto you." (Matthew 6:33). Seeking after fleshly and earthly things instead of pursuing after the things of our Creator will bring chaos in our lives. God wants to have a relationship with His creations so He can lead us into the pathway of abundant life. He is my strong tower, He is my defense, and He is my refuge at all times. What is He to you?

CHAPTER 4: CHALLENGING TIMES

Drinking alcohol and smoking were the norm. This became my way of life, but I still did not find happiness. During the first years of separation, friends such as the late Mary Dorsett (May her soul rest in peace) and Christine Fernander were very instrumental; they were there for support. Their kindness will never be forgotten.

In 1991, I divorced my husband. The children were still in his care. As I reflect on the situation, that was a very trying time for me emotionally. Neither of us was ready for marriage from the beginning, and it was doomed for failure. The divorce process was very painful, and I had no family support since they thought I was at fault and Nod was perfect. All I could do was cry for comfort.

Are you in a troubled marriage? Seek professional counseling and direction from God through prayer and becoming intimate with Him through His word. I was in captivity for ten years. It was God's grace and mercy that kept me with a sound mind. I drank alcohol day and night for comfort. I did not realize it then, but only intimacy with our Creator God brings us absolute comfort and peace. I struggled for a very long time with self-confidence since I thought I had failed in my life, and that was it for me. However, as time progressed, I believed in myself and realized that life does not end after a divorce. You have to believe in yourself when no one else believes in you and know you can survive any challenges.

In 1992, my ex-husband finally accepted I was not returning and decided he would let me have my girls.

Even though I was not aware of God's plans and destiny for my life, His love and compassion kept me for a purpose. "Through the Lord's mercies, we are not consumed because his compassions fail not. They are new every morning; great is your faithfulness." (Lamentations 3:22-23). Whatever challenge you are facing right now, you can overcome it with your faith in God. Do not focus on the situation, see God as being greater! The purpose of your pain is to bring you out to a wealthy place.

Have faith in Jehovah Shalom, the God of peace. Greatness is your portion if you believe.

CHAPTER 5: A NEW LIFE

April 16, 1994, was the year I finally made a sobering decision to surrender my life to Jesus. My co-worker and I had an invitation to attend my cousin's wedding in Nassau, Bahamas. Two days prior to this event, I was drinking in the nightclub, trying to forget all my problems. We left for Nassau the day before the wedding, and I was well. During the wedding ceremony, as the bride made her entrance at the door of the church to walk down the aisle, the spirit of death came upon me. I felt my spirit leaving my body, and immediately, fear gripped me. I never mentioned to my friend what was happening to me. I wanted to tell her to call an ambulance, but I was frozen in fear. I could not comprehend what was happening around me.

I remember praying in my heart, "Please do not let me die in my sins". We traveled back to Eleuthera on the same day as the wedding. On our way to the airport, I revealed to my friend what I had experienced. She could not understand the feeling of death I was trying to explain. At this time, I was losing all focus, yet I had not received Jesus into my heart. Two days later, in the comfort of my bedroom, I confessed my sins and asked Jesus to come into my life. I felt a sense of peace come upon me.

The Lord knew my beginning and He knew my end, so He knew I was not going to die but live to declare His goodness to others. Sometimes, we have to experience unusual circumstances to surrender our lives to the Lord. He died that we may have life—and have it more abundantly.

Shortly after returning to Eleuthera, the Assemblies of God Church in Rock Sound, Eleuthera was having two weeks of revival services with an Evangelist from Freeport, Bahamas, as the guest speaker. I believe God sent him just for me. Those feelings I experienced at my cousin's wedding gripped me with fear once again. As the evangelist preached the word of God, this was the beginning of my breakthrough.

The spirit of death continued to torment me. Every morning, I read the Psalms; my favorite was Psalm 91. I did not understand what was happening to me, but I cried out unto the Lord, and He heard me. I often caught my girls staring at me, wondering what was happening to their mother. I could not explain to them what I was experiencing. I had lost a lot of weight because my appetite was gone. Gossip was going around that I had some type of incurable disease. Oh, if they only knew what I was experiencing. But I could not explain it. God knew, and that was all that mattered. And thankfully, He promised to never leave me alone.

The Lord impressed upon my heart to leave the rented apartment where I was living and move somewhere else. One Saturday morning, as I was doing my house chores the phone rang. It was a friend telling me I should move out of the apartment as soon as I could. She did not know I was making plans to move, so I knew this was God confirming what He had impressed upon my heart. Within a week, I moved into a rented house. Those feelings of death still continued to haunt me, but I kept praying to God to have mercy on me. I also kept reading the word of God because His word is life. I read and meditated on the scriptures throughout the days.

This process lasted nineteen months. However, God carried me through as He carried the children of Israel through the wilderness. During these most difficult days, a very close friend was a great source of encouragement and support. God had divinely brought her into my life some years prior. We became close friends when I was drinking and carousing. Even though she did not carouse as I did, she was not ashamed to associate with me. My family did not know what I was going through and I did not think they would have understood anyway. I felt so rejected and did not care to discuss my situation with them.

God often uses us during adverse circumstances to be an encouragement to others. While I was employed with the National Insurance Board (the social security agency of the Bahamas) in Rock Sound, Eleuthera, I had the opportunity to minister one-on-one to people from all walks of life. I never got so engrossed in my circumstances that I could not reach out to others who needed help. However, at tough times I felt as if God had turned His back on me and

I was in the world alone. "Many are the afflictions of the righteous, but the Lord delivers him out of them all." (Psalm 34:19) When Job was so greatly afflicted, instead of complaining against God, he worshipped. He lost everything he possessed, and lastly, his body was afflicted. In all of his tribulations, he still maintained his integrity.

What challenges are you facing right now? I admonish you to believe in God and know that after you have suffered a while, you will be made perfect, established, strengthened and settled. God assured me through His written word, prophetic utterance, and dreams that He was with me. One night, I had a dream that I was in my grandmother's house in Bannerman Town, and suddenly I looked up and saw two big airplanes flying over the house in a circular motion as if they were going to crash. I was so afraid in the dream and all of a sudden, an angel appeared flying around the house, also in a circular motion. God was assuring me of His divine protection, no matter what.

CHAPTER 6: TESTING TIMES

One night, I received a long-distance call from a woman of God whom I had not heard from in a long time. She called to say that the Lord told her to bless me with her home, which was vacant at the time. I was renting, the landlord was exceptionally nice, very kind and understanding. I was making plans to eventually ask her to let me purchase her home. However, I felt this woman's offer had to be a blessing from God. I was young in my walk with the Lord, and even though I was stunned to hear this, I thought it was God. The enemy will always try to destroy the plans God has for our lives. "The thief does not come except to steal, and to kill and to destroy. I have come that they may have life and that they may have it more abundantly." (John 10:10). I battled in my mind about how I was going to discuss my decision to move on such short notice with the landlord. I eventually told her my decision to move; she was disappointed and begged me not to go. What I did not know was that hell was waiting for me.

Everyone that comes to you and says, "Thus says the Lord," is not speaking on God's behalf. The prophet Jeremiah cautions us about false prophets. Remember, people speaking on God's behalf should be a confirmation of what God has already told you. As Christians, we should always ask the Holy Spirit to increase our discernment and always be sensitive to His leadership. Once I settled in the woman's house, I found out it needed many repairs, and she wanted me to give her money for staying there. I had been deceived but could not move again because I had exhausted all my finances. I had to sell a piece of property I had intended to build on so I could pay her the money she asked for and cover the repairs on the house. During those great tests and trials, I maintained my integrity and relationship with God. Through all the confusion, hurt, disappointment, and sleepless nights, I kept a smile on my face.

The scripture declares, "Blessed be the God and father of our Lord Jesus Christ, the father of mercies and God of all comfort who comforts us in all our tribulation that we may be able to comfort those who are in any trouble with the comfort which we ourselves are comforted by God." (II Corinthians 1:3-4)

Eventually, some family disputes over this supposed blessing from the Lord came up, and I had to pack up and move again. This time, I faced more "hell". My pastor at the time had heard of my circumstances and given me permission to move into the church mission house. The enemy did not like this, and within a couple of months, rumors were out that I was having an affair with the pastor. This rumor devastated me because it was not true. Despite it being untrue, I was given notice by my pastor to move out within two weeks. I had no idea where my younger daughter and I were going to live. My older daughter was away in college in the U.S.A.

I stayed away from the ministry I attended for three months because of the deep hurt I experienced. I never had a meeting with my pastor to resolve the situation. However, I maintained my relationship with God and discovered that He is the only one who never fails. The word of God declares, "It is better to trust in the Lord than to put confidence in man." (Psalms 118:8). Church folk will hurt you with an everlasting hurt that only God can erase. Fortunately, God will always have someone in place for us; He will not leave us defenseless. Never put your trust in the arms of flesh; you will be greatly disappointed. Only God never fails us. Within a week, I had moved into the rented house of a friend's family and lived rent-free for a few months. I learned from this that God would put people in our lives for purpose and destiny. My daughter and I did not lack anything; we were treated as part of the family. This had been my fourth time moving from place to place. Could you imagine the gossip that raised its ugly head again? I kept on smiling despite what I was going through. God has our future in His hands. However, we have to trust Him with it.

A faithful friend stood by my side when no one else but God was there. Her family was like my family. They were great emotional support for me. Only God can reward their kindness. A few months after moving, I felt the need to move again because I did not want to be a burden on that family. Again, I moved into another "hell hole" of trials. Many times in our lives, we have to go through trials and errors before we finally arrive at our predestined place. The house I moved into was not in good condition, and I believe that because of my need for a place, I was taken advantage of again. I was emotionally drained; however, I always had a smile. The months I spent in the rented house were another challenging time for me. The landlord was not compassionate at all. She did not have much patience when I tried to explain some unfortunate situations I was going through. I wanted to give up on life, but God's grace and mercy kept me sane. I was weary and torn apart, I cried out

to God, "Oh God, not again!" Jesus told Peter, "Simon, Simon! Indeed Satan has asked for you that he may sift you as wheat. But I have prayed for you; that your faith should not fail and when you have returned to me, strengthen your brethren." (Luke 22: 31-32) When we endure trials, we are qualified to help bring other people through.

Looking back at all of this, God was working it out for my good. I used these tests as a stepping-stone for moving forward into my divine destiny. A friend whom I looked up to as a mentor eventually encouraged me to return to the ministry. I took her advice and went back with my usual smile. These situations taught me how to minister to others faced with similar situations. I did not allow hate or animosity to come into my heart. I ministered and served faithfully. I always wanted to know that others around me were happy even when I was having a challenging day. And I never stopped smiling.

As you are reading this book, right now, you may be faced with some impossible situations or your life may be stagnant. There is hope for you! Work your dreams and visions along with faith in God. What you need for your breakthrough is locked up inside you. I declare over now, and you are coming out of captivity into a wealthy place! God's servant Job lost everything he owned; he lost his health, wealth, and family from his severe trial. But he emerged with a fresh appreciation of God's sovereignty and sufficiency. In his later years, God blessed him double for his trouble. Continue to trust God.

CHAPTER 7: A TURN-AROUND

It was during the year 1998 that I answered the call of God to preach the gospel. Earlier in my Christian walk; I knew that God was calling me to be one of his mouthpieces on earth. My first message was entitled "Where art thou?" taken from Genesis 3:9. My heart's desire is to minister to the broken and the lost. We must forsake all and follow Jesus wholeheartedly. God is calling out a remnant of people who will hear His voice and obey. His remnant is anointed by the Holy Spirit to preach the gospel to the poor, preach deliverance to the captives, preach the acceptable year of the Lord, heal the brokenhearted, recover sight to the blind, and set at liberty them that are in bondage. Allow God to make you over for effective service in His kingdom.

In the summer of 1999, I moved again. The house had become unlivable. This was my seventh time moving. A friend assisted me with moving again. She was always a true friend. True friends do not change when you are faced with difficulties or challenges. This time. I moved into her brother's home, who was away in school. Some folks had a problem with me moving among this family. Always know people will gossip about you, but your destiny is in God's hands. Never allow pressure to sidetrack you from your purpose. As I went through those difficult days, my faith in God grew, and I remained focused. When we put our total trust in God, we shall never be ashamed or confounded. Faith not tested is not faith at all.

I served faithfully in the ministry I attended despite the setbacks I encountered. There was always a big smile on my face. God rewards faithfulness, and whatever you sow, you will reap in due season. In addition to serving in the local church, I served for five years as the President of Lord's Ladies Ministry International, founded by Dr. Sybil Whitenburg of Columbia, South Carolina. Those were challenging years serving as President because I did not have any leadership experience. Dr. Whitenburg and other seasoned women of God in the Bahamas, such as Minister Colamae Collymore of Bahamas Faith Ministries, Nassau, New Providence and Evangelist Shirley Burrows of Living Word

Ministries, Governor's Harbor, Eleuthera, helped shape me for leadership. My pastor and his wife were also instrumental in developing my leadership abilities.

My tenure was an opportunity to be a servant to those who were under my leadership. I served with joy and excitement even though my mind battled for a while over my self-confidence. I felt like I was not qualified and equipped to lead, but Jesus calls them underqualified and qualifies them for service in His kingdom. My leadership role opened up doors for me to travel locally and internationally with Evangelist Collymore. She was fun to travel with and I also learned a lot about different aspects of ministry. I gleaned wisdom "nuggets," which helped me to stay focused on the journey. It is very vital as a young believer to associate yourself with mature men and women of God; they can help you walk through difficult times in ministry and avoid many pitfalls.

During the year 2000, my hunger for spiritual things increased, and I desired a more intimate relationship with God. As believers, everything that concerns our life is tied to our intimacy with our Creator. Our human nature is after material things instead of the Kingdom's agenda. Matthew 6 33 admonishes us as believers to seek the kingdom of God first. All through my trials and tests, I knew that purpose and destiny were calling out to me. You need mental toughness to reach your destiny. Sometimes you will have to forsake family and friends in order to fulfill your purpose for being on the earth. Distraction is a thief to keep you stagnant. People who always thought my destiny was in their hands often criticized me. I learned a valuable lesson in life: if you have a vision for your life, very seldom will you be sidetracked. Vision keeps you focused in the face of challenging times. The Webster's dictionary defines "vision" as 1. A power of seeing, 2. Something seen in a dream, trance, etc., 3. A mental image, 4. Foresight.

What are you seeing in your life? You are never too old to fulfil your life's purpose and destiny. The story of Zacharias and Elizabeth in Luke Chapter 1 is a perfect example of staying focused on what God instructs us to do. "As Zacharias the priest performed his priestly duties, the angel of the Lord appeared unto him and said, "Do not be afraid, Zacharias, for your prayer is heard and your wife Elizabeth will bear you a son, and you shall call his name John." When the full time had come for her to conceive, she brought forth a son as was promised by the angel of the Lord. Her neighbors and relatives rejoiced with her. The time came for the child to be circumcised, and they wanted to name him after his father, Zacharias." Elizabeth was bold enough to say no, he shall be called John, as told to Zacharias by the angel. They were upset because no one in the family was called by that name. Divine destiny was in the name of John because he came as a forerunner before Christ. It is better to obey God rather than man. God has a plan for us as well as our generation. God is raising a remnant of believers as Kings and Priests all over the world who will decree and declare a thing, and it shall be established. Are you a part of that remnant? Are you fulfilling your God-given assignment? Obedience is better than sacrifice. Step out in faith and impact lives for the Kingdom of God.

CHAPTER 8: MOVING FORWARD

In 2001, the Holy Spirit began to impress upon my heart to leave Eleuthera, the island of my birth. I began to make mental preparations for the transition. Sometimes, when God speaks, we may have to wait for further instructions and confirmation. We should ensure it lines up with His word. The word of God is the final authority over our lives. His word is forever settled in heaven and His faithfulness is unto all generations. We are a part of all generations. When the Holy Spirit dealt with my heart to transition to Nassau, I was careful of whom I shared it with because most people will discourage you from moving forward in your predestined purpose. In addition, some believers will try to intimidate you and make you believe that only they can hear God speak. All of God's children should hear from Him for direction for their lives if we are intimate with Him. I had to disconnect my association with negative persons and connect with positive persons during my transition.

When 2002 came, God made a sudden shift in my life. I had to make some major decisions that would affect my life forever. I received the peace of the Lord that my season was finished in Rock Sound, Eleuthera. When God impresses upon your heart to transition from one city to another, obey His leading. Do not miss your divine destiny. My confirmation was God's peace and His word, "Now the Lord had said to Abram: Get out of your country, from your family and from your father's house, to a land that I will show you. I will make you a great nation, I will bless you and make your name great, and you shall be a blessing. I will bless those who bless you, and I will curse him who curses you, and in you, all the families of the earth shall be blessed." (Genesis 1: 1-3) The blessings of the Lord are connected to our faith and obedience.

I requested a transfer to Nassau, and my superiors denied the request. I was upset and wondered why I was denied the transfer. However, I dwelt in the peace of the Lord. God's ways are not like our ways; His thoughts are not like our thoughts. The Holy Spirit spoke to me one morning as I sat at my desk at work. I heard these words clearly, "If you do not move now, you will miss me!" On August 23, 2002, I said goodbye to 20 years of service with the National Insurance Board (the social security agency of the Bahamas), a career I held dear to my heart. I was leaving behind co-workers, my church family, and the people I served for all those years. However, God was ordering my steps, and I had to obey. The scripture declares, "Trust in the Lord will all of your heart, and lean not on your own understanding; in all your ways acknowledge him and he shall direct your paths." (Proverbs 3: 5-6) As I trusted in the Lord, my faith was being increased each day. Without faith, it is impossible to please God. If you are walking in disobedience and fear, you are missing God's blessing for your life.

On August 30, 2002, I left Eleuthera for the big city of Nassau. I gave up all the comfort and the serenity of the island life to begin a journey of faith. I knew my divine destiny was in my obedience. What is God speaking in your heart concerning your destiny? Are you afraid to leave your comfortable environment? It took a lot of courage for Abraham to leave home at the age of 75, not knowing where he was going. The Lord spoke to Abraham's spirit, but he had to walk it out in the flesh. There are some things we have to do in order to fulfil our purpose. Throughout Abraham's journey of faith, he built an altar and worshipped His creator. Purpose and destiny resulted from Abraham's obedience to move away from home. His family practiced idolatry, and there were wicked sinners all around him. If he stayed, it would be hard for Abraham to live for God and be pure. Through Abraham's seed came the Savior of the world. If I had focused on my challenges, I would have never obeyed the leading of the Lord. Transition is never easy on the flesh because you will go through periods of feeling alone. However, with God, we are never alone. There were many times when the enemy tried to torment my mind, telling me that I did not have a future. It took a lot of faith, courage, and a renewed mindset for me to stay focused.

When I arrived in Nassau, I lived with my mom. This was a challenge because my mom and I were not getting along as mother and daughter. She was very upset with me because I had resigned from my job and left a good career. She told me that I would suffer and not progress in life. I was hurt by these words, but yet I continued with a smile on my face.

Words spoken are life or death, and those words were not life. However, I prayed against every negative word spoken over my life. God has given us the authority to come against the plans of the enemy concerning our lives. I refused to allow anyone to dictate my life according to what he/she thought it should be like. As I matured in Christ and studied the word of God, I found out who I am in Him. The written word of God is the final authority to every situation that you are faced with, not what friends or family say. When you walk in faith and obedience, there is a price to pay; you will be misunderstood. God gave me His assurance that He was with me. When God challenges us to step out from the familiar to the unfamiliar, we cannot rely on what we see or how we feel. We should stand on God's word. God is bigger than any situation we will ever encounter. The adversary's assignment is to have us focused on the problems. "Blessed be the God and father of our Lord Jesus Christ, the father of mercies and God of all comfort, who comforts us in all our tribulation that we may be able to comfort those who are in any trouble, with the comfort with which we ourselves are comforted by God." (II Corinthians 1: 3-4)

One of my greatest challenges was trying to adjust to living with my mom. I was the head of my home for sixteen years after I divorced my ex-husband. I was used to doing things my way and having my own privacy. God will put us in uncomfortable situations to build character and patience in us. Are you willing to allow the crucibles of life to make you over for God's honor and glory? Each day I encouraged myself in the Lord. Some persons that I thought would be there to help encourage me in my process were not there for me. I was misunderstood so many times. Most people never accept change in your life. However, nothing remains the same for as long as you live. I admonish you today: embrace your season of change and go through the process of life. Many blessings await you.

CHAPTER 9: THE NEXT MOVE

I lived with Mom for three weeks until a friend persuaded me to move in with her and her husband. This was a way of escape since I did not have a bond with my mom, and she was still upset with me for leaving my job. I packed up and left.

However, things did not work out well with that couple, so after a few weeks, I asked my sister, Georgan, if I could move in with her. She did not hesitate to have me move in with her and my niece Kendrell and nephew Kendrick Jr. She was happy with this move because I helped her care for my niece and nephew. During those days, I was employed at an insurance company and a bakery for a while. This made it possible for me to contribute to the household as best as possible.

My sister and I got along well even though we had many confrontations. It was difficult to communicate with her at times because I did not grow up with her and my other sister. Sometimes, I felt like I was living with a complete stranger. If you are a parent reading this book, if possible, let your children grow up together. It is not wise to separate children between you and grandparents or others.

Even though I lived with my sister, I visited my mom regularly. It did not help much, and I still felt distant from her. God always has a way to work things out according to His perfect will for our lives. In 2004, my mom had an appointment with her physician for her regular physical check-up. One test result revealed Stage II breast cancer. I had accompanied her when she went for the test results. I watched in shock as my mom cried when her doctor gave her those results. I placed my hand on her shoulder and tried to console her. She quickly composed herself as the doctor went on to tell her about the options she had for survival. She had to have a left breast mastectomy. This news was devastating to her and the entire family. Words could not describe my feelings regarding my mom being diagnosed with a life-threatening illness.

After I left the doctor's office, I went back to Georgan's, packed my belongings, and left her house to move in with Mom to take care of her. Georgan agreed with this decision. I did not know the challenges my mom would face, but this was the beginning of our bond, if only for a short time. She was scheduled to receive aggressive chemotherapy treatments immediately because the cancer was very aggressive. The first two treatments made her very sick, so she refused to complete the third treatment. The days and weeks went by, and Mom seemed to be progressing well. She decided she would try natural products to help her get better.

I thought moving in with Mom again was going to be a challenge. However, we began interacting with each other, and it was a relief to me. I came to find out more than anything else Mom loved me a lot. In the past, she did not know how to express her feelings. We laughed, cooked together, and sat on her patio almost every day. In addition to that, we took care of my sister's children, whom she loved dearly. I took care of all the daily chores so that she could relax and live a stress-free life. As we bonded, she apologized for the negative words she had spoken, and she said blessings to my children and me. Daily, she expressed how much she appreciated the way I was taking care of her and helping out with her grandchildren.

In June of 2005, Mom's cancer went into remission. I decided I needed a change of atmosphere, so I contacted a couple I knew in Columbia, South Carolina.

They were connected with a Bible College in Detroit, Michigan. I always wanted to attend Bible College and I felt this was an open door to get away for a while. This news did not go well with mom, but I needed a change. She did not want me to go. Her philosophy was always to have her family close by her side. Despite how she felt, I packed up and left the Bahamas permanently, or so I thought (I did not indicate this to Mom).

I spent eight financially challenging months in South Carolina. This was walking by faith. However, God supernaturally provided for me in ways I could not comprehend. I did not attend Bible College and instead got involved with a wonderful ministry and church family. They treated me with honor. I called Mom regularly to see how she was doing. Each time, she would ask when I was coming back home to Nassau, and my reply was "soon." However, the move for me was refreshing and I did not plan to return.

In December of that same year, I left South Carolina to spend the Christmas and New Year's holidays with my girls in Jacksonville, Florida. While I was there, I received some devastating news from Nassau that my cousin's husband had been killed. I made plans to attend the funeral. Latanya and I made a surprise visit home to the Bahamas. Mom was overjoyed to see us. In fact, all the family members were happy that I was home despite the sad occasion. I stayed home for three months after the funeral, and Mom was so happy.

Mom had a doctor's appointment on the same day I left Nassau, so I decided to stay in Jacksonville to await the results instead of going directly back to South Carolina. Later on that night, I called Mom; the news was not good. Tumors had developed in the area where she had the mastectomy. Mom sounded very strong in spirit on the phone, and I encouraged her that God was still with her. Two days later my sister called to say that Mom requested that I come back home to help her with the grandchildren after school. I will be very honest and forthcoming. I did not want to return. I called my pastor in South Carolina to discuss the situation. She encouraged me to honor Mom's request by going back home. I felt like my world was torn apart. "And we know that all things work together for the good of those who love God, to those who are the called according to his purpose." (Romans 8:28) Many times in our lives, we may not always understand the process of transitions that we go through, however it is God's purpose and plan for our lives. Are you willing to submit to God's will and do away with your will?

Mom's cancer came back with a vengeance, and chemotherapy treatments were her only hope of survival. She agreed to have the treatments even though it made her very sick and all of her hair fell out. Mom cried when this first happened and I looked with pain in my heart.

I had so many unanswered questions for God. Mom's faith in God was firm, and she believed He would heal her. As I write this section of the book, I am emotional because this brings back so many memories of Mom's illness. Mom ministered to so many people about God's faithfulness during her most difficult days. Her unwavering faith in God encouraged her family and friends when they came by to see her. She read the word of God consistently; this was her daily comfort.

As Mom's condition got worse, Aunt Eulita and I were back and forth with her for doctors' visits. Some days, she was strong in spirit, and some days, she was so weak. She never complained but gave God glory in the affliction. I saw in Mom tenacity, faith, and hope. Many nights, the pain in her left arm was unbearable, but she always called on the name of Jesus. I continuously laid my hands on Mom, prayed and encouraged her through God's word. Mom also had strong emotional and spiritual support from her two brothers, George and Alexander, her niece, Deneria and other family members and friends. Mom had a great love for God, her church family and especially her six grandchildren, Latanya, Lindsay, Kendrell, Kendrick, Jonathan and Olivia.

The chemotherapy treatments were not helping the spread of the cancer, and in April 2006, Mom was hospitalized for two weeks due to respiratory problems. This was when we learned the cancer was Stage IV, and there was no hope for survival. We did not disclose this news to her but rested in the assurance that God would heal her. Mom was discharged from the hospital and continued with her life, having some good days and some bad days. In September 2006, Mom's health began to deteriorate. She became weaker in body but not in spirit. She still wanted to cook her favorite meal and care for her grandchildren. This was a part of her life before she became ill, and she wanted to continue it. I stayed up with Mom many nights when she experienced excruciating pain in her left arm. I continued to pray and encourage her from the Word of God. She would cry out to God and often times she would fall asleep.

One of Mom's attending physicians wanted to meet with my sisters and one of my cousins about her failing health. I was not at the meeting because I was in Jacksonville, Florida, visiting my girls for the Thanksgiving holiday. They received heartbreaking news at the meeting. Mom's estimated remaining time was only six months to a year. Despite this news, we continued to believe the report of the Lord. God's report says we are healed by the stripes of Jesus.

CHAPTER 10: PERFECT PEACE

Our family usually got together for fellowship during the Christmas and New Year's holidays. In 2006, it was different. Mom made all the decisions as to where we should gather for breakfast and dinner and requested certain family members to attend. We gathered at cousin Deneria's home for Christmas dinner, and mom was excited to have her family gathered around her. On New Year's 2007 morning, we gathered at Cousin Harriet's home for breakfast. Mom enjoyed herself relaxing at the poolside with her beloved family, especially her grandchildren. My children were the only ones not present. Mom wanted to help in the kitchen, but I was insisted that she sit and relax. This she did reluctantly. I really did not think that this would be my mother's last holiday with us. She was always family oriented and the matriarch in our family, so this did not seem out of the ordinary.

When we left Cousin Harriet's home, Mom took to bed complaining of not feeling well. I thought she over-exhausted herself and needed some rest. However, as the days in January 2007 went by, Mom's health weakened. Her appetite was minimal each day. I tried to force her to eat, but all she wanted most of the time was a cup of hot tea. This was a concern for the family, but we thought she would be okay.

I had to attend a speaking engagement at the "Women of Purpose" conference held in Rock Sound, Eleuthera. I decided to leave a few days earlier and left Mom in the care of my sisters, Georgan and Leila, and Mom's sister, Aunt Eulita. I called Mom every day to see how she was feeling, and each time she would respond, she was fine, but I knew in my spirit it was not well with her. As soon as the conference was over, I returned to care for Mom. When I arrived from the airport and got inside the house, my mom was lying on her side, almost lifeless. By her side was her cousin Rubliee and niece Deneria. I asked Mom how she was feeling, and she replied, "Not well". I could not accept the reality that Mom was soon to leave us. In the days following, Mom kept telling me thanks for all I had done for her during her illness and that God would always bless me. On February 1, 2007, at about 10 am, one of her nurses from the oncology clinic called the house to get some information that she needed. I answered the phone and told her I did not like the way Mom was breathing, and she suggested I bring her to the accident and emergency department quickly. When I hung up the phone, I told Mom what the nurse had said, and she was willing to go. I got her dressed and called Georgan and Leila at work to let them know we needed to take Mom to the hospital. Leila left work immediately to take us to the hospital. Mom was admitted, but she was very ill. I noticed a change in her face; it looked very dry and pale. Mom was only 68 years old. However, her life was in God's hands.

Mom's body was so weakened she needed assistance to use the restroom and help with her daily baths. All through this change, she remained peaceful, praising and giving God thanks. We visited her every day, and each time I saw Mom, she was not getting better. Her desire for food was no longer there. I had to clean Mom up while she was lying in bed. She was too weak to move with her own ability. We informed family and friends that Mom was not doing well and that they should visit her.

Sunday, February 4, 2007, Mom's bedside was overflowing with loved ones, including her church family. She embraced everyone with much love and smile, trying to put her best side out. This would be the last time they saw her alive. I went back to the hospital the next day to spend some time with Mom. She was just lying on her back very pale, but yet with a smile when she saw me. Only God understood what I felt each time I went by her bedside. I sat with her for a while, and we conversed with each other. She never indicated she was leaving us.

On February 6, Leila and I went to the hospital early because the doctors told us she would be released to come home under the condition of being kept on an oxygen tank to support her breathing. We still were hoping Mom would survive for a while longer. A team of doctors wanted to meet with us before we took her home. We met and they informed us that Mom was very ill. As we listened, both of us prepared for the worst news...they could do nothing else to keep Mom alive. Leila went back into the room to spend some time with Mom, but I could not go. I was too devastated by the doctors' report.

We had already informed Georgan and the rest of the family and friends that Mom was being discharged. Due to her weak condition, she could not breathe without the oxygen tank and had to be transported by ambulance. We left the hospital to go home and await the arrival of Mom. However, Leila wanted me to take her to her apartment so she could finish helping her husband with their packing to move into their new home. I kept her car and went back to Mom's house to wait for her arrival. Every time I called the hospital to check when she would be home, they gave me a different time. After 5 p.m., I was concerned and called Georgan, who was still at work, to stop by the hospital to check on Mom. I stayed at home with my nieces and nephews. Gradually, people came by the house looking for Mom. The phone rang, and Georgan was on the other line, telling me to come to the hospital quickly. I left the children with a friend and made my way to the hospital. I prayed and asked the Lord for strength to face the unexpected.

When I arrived at the hospital, my heart was aching, and I was speechless. Upon my arrival at her bedside, her breath was leaving her frail body. I looked her all over and began to rub her forehead. The feelings I experienced cannot be described; tears could not come. I kept pacing up and down around her bedside as everyone looked at Mom in disbelief. One of her nurses came by to ask us to leave and wait outside the room. Not long after, we heard a code over the intercom. We knew for sure this call was for doctors to come and pronounce Mom officially dead. Doctors came running past us, and within minutes, they came back to tell us that Mom had passed. We looked at each other in disbelief and shock.

Leila and her husband, Rev. Harvey Cash, were still busy moving into their new home. We finally made phone contact with them, and they joined us at the hospital. We called for the family mortician to take the remains of our mom, and we left the hospital to gather at Mom's home. We had a long night calling people and receiving loved ones and friends at Mom's home. Everyone was quiet, trying to come to terms with the reality that Mom was no longer with us. The moment was sobering. Mom was the matriarch of our family and a friend and confidant to many.

During the course of preparation for the funeral, our home was flooded with people from all walks of society, people whom we did not know or had not seen in years. We realized the impact Mom made on the lives of people while she was alive. Mom also touched the political arena in an indelible way. The Prime Minister of the Commonwealth of the Bahamas at that time was the Honorable Perry Christie. He had called her home on several occasions when she was ill to see how she was doing.

We made preparations for the funeral with mixed emotions. We were happy that she went home to be with the Lord and sad that she left us so soon. Family and friends came from all over the USA and the Bahamas to attend Mom's homegoing service. As time got nearer the funeral day, we were extremely busy entertaining the flow of people coming in to show homage to our beloved mother, aunt, grandmother, sister, cousin and friend to so many. The funeral was held on February 14 at 10 am at the Church of God Convention Center on Yamacraw Road. Family and friends, including Mom's adopted son, Edgar Curling, and his wife Beverly, assembled at the house to await the arrival of the limousines. We waited with soberness until it was time to leave the house to go to the church where Mom's remains were laid out.

A throng of family members and well wishes were assembled, awaiting our arrival.

The funeral director prayed as we got out of each limousine. He then led us to view the remains of our beloved. This was a very difficult moment; however, God strengthened us to face this most difficult time of our lives. The God of all comfort comforts us in all our sorrows so that we may be able to comfort those who go through the same things. The funeral services proceeded with a time of praise and thanksgiving. This was a way of life for Mom all during her illness. I kept strong for my children and sisters. Georgan, Edgar and Leila gave tribute in song and special moments, and I read from the scriptures. The

Prime Minister brought greetings on behalf of the government of the Commonwealth of the Bahamas, along with the Honorable Kenyatta Gibson, the representative for the constituency where Mom lived. Other ministers of religion paid special tribute, and her beloved Bishop Moses Johnson eulogized her.

The time came for us to leave with the body and go to her final resting place. Many well-wishers surrounded us and offered encouragement before we left for the gravesite. It was at this time I broke down in tears. Mom had left us, and now it was a reality. On the way to the cemetery, I was quiet and almost in a trance-like state of mind. At times, I wondered if this was really happening or if I was dreaming. If I did not have a relationship with the Lord, I do not know how I would have made it through Mom's illness and her subsequent death. God allowed me to endure with a strength that I did not know I had.

At the gravesite, we each took our seats under the tents with Mom's grave facing us. I held on to my nephew, Kendrick, as he wanted to look into the grave. He was diagnosed with down syndrome and was very special to Mom. Georgan and Leila had to be consoled. After the short graveside service, we returned to the limousines and headed home. At the house, we had a celebration with food and drinks and reminisced on different events that occurred while Mom was with us. Laughter filled the air. Mom would have wanted the celebration.

As the days and weeks went by, we tried to cope with the fact that Mom was no longer physically in our midst but only in our thoughts and mind. I would not hear her calling out my name to make her a cup of tea or letting me know how much she appreciated me taking good care of her. I had to pick up my life and gradually move on with my purpose and destiny. So many times, people get stuck in situations and circumstances that are designed to bring you out into your predestined place. God is always perfecting the things that concern us and He never tells us how He will do it. We have to trust Him for each step of the journey of life.

The Lord is ordering my steps, and I am submissive to His will for my life. I encourage you to go on and embrace all your seasons of change!

CHAPTER 11: FAITH FOR THE NEXT MOVE

I spent a few weeks in Nassau after Mom passed, and then packed up and left the Bahamas upon the leading of the Holy Spirit. My family had mixed emotions about me leaving home to transition to Jacksonville, Florida. Some thought I should have stayed and found employment. However, I chose to obey the leading of the Lord. My daughters were anxiously awaiting my arrival at the Orlando International Airport. We were excited to see each other again after such a sad occasion. They loved their grandmother dearly.

Upon arriving, I received the good news that I was soon to be a grandmother. I was elated! The transition into Jacksonville required total trust in God. Imagine adjusting to a new culture. Even though both of my daughters lived there, I still had to find my own way. I learned throughout my life that it requires faith to leave everything familiar behind and move forward into the unfamiliar. Abraham, in Genesis 12, is a perfect example of having child-like faith. He was an old man, 75 years old. However, he obeyed God when he was told to leave the familiarity and go to a land that he knew not of. I imagine Abraham saying to God, "But who is going to carry on my legacy back home because I have no son, and besides, I am already too old to go anywhere. The people in my town are going to think I lost my mind and besides, my family will never agree with me in this move." Does this sound like something you said to God about moving into a new place? Note that Abraham's story ends with perpetual blessings affecting generations even today. The walk of faith creates an atmosphere for unusual provision and blessings. We will never know "Elohim", mighty or strong one, or Jehovah Shalom, "The Lord is Peace", if we stay in our comfortable place.

As I settled in Jacksonville, I had to depend totally on God and not on what I was feeling or what I was seeing. I stood firm on the word of God, which is forever settled in heaven. Are you fulfilling your purpose in the earth? Before you were born, you were on the mind of God. He created you uniquely from everyone else. Do not let fear and intimidation keep you stagnant. They are enemies of our soul. Wherever you are situated, you are there to effect change in your sphere of influence. You have the power within you to make a marked difference in the lives of people from all walks of life. Arise and move into your God-given assignment. You will never know what is in you until you submit your will totally to God's will for your life.

As I was going through the different challenges in my life, I knew God's hand was upon me. His thoughts toward me were of peace and not of evil, to give me a future and hope (Jeremiah 29:11). I am progressing in my purpose and destiny and have no regrets for all that I have been through. Paul declares, "Yet in all these things we are more than conquerors through Him who loved us. I am persuaded that neither death nor life, nor angels nor principalities nor powers, nor things present nor things to come, nor height nor depth nor any other created thing, shall be able to separate us from the love of God which is in Christ Jesus our Lord." (Romans 8:37-39)

Move on in your God-given purpose and be all that God created you to be on the earth. Greatness is your portion!

IN APPRECIATION

First and foremost, thank you to the Sovereign God, Jesus my redeemer and precious Holy Spirit who inspired me to write this book.

Thanks to my wonderful daughters Latanya and Lindsay. You both encouraged and motivated me in the things of the Lord. You both helped to push me into my God-given purpose. Many blessings await your new destiny in God!

To my grandson Brayden, you bring so much happiness to my life. You are a leader in your generation.

To my sisters Georgan and Leila, I thank God for both of you. Greatness is your portion!

To my wonderful friends Margarita Symonette Hill, Gertrude Saunders, Marcia Seymour, Shannelle Johnson, Donna Davis, Melvina Poitier, Brenda Bethel, Prophetess Violet Thompson, Evangelist Alice Ferguson, Susan Domianos, Minister Dianne Ingraham and Janet Dohanue. You all have greatly impacted my life in some way. May great grace be upon you all in your endeavors!

To the "Symonettes", my adopted family, words alone cannot express my deep appreciation and sincere thanks for the outpouring of love and support to my family and me. May your barns overflow with blessings and favor?

Evangelist Shirley Burrows and Minister Colamae Collymore, thanks for all of the encouragement and wisdom nuggets you imparted in my life. May you continue to contend for the Faith!

To Carol Scriven for editing and designing the book cover.

ABOUT THE AUTHOR

Gaylean Maynard (born Gaylean Sharon Brown-Maynard) is a Bahamian author, speaker, and religious figure known for her books that focus on her spiritual journey and her message of triumph through faith. She is described as a woman of faith with a passion for people and a desire to advance the Kingdom of God. She has also been interviewed on television programs, where she has shared her experiences in the religious sphere, particularly in her role as an Apostle.

Authorship: Maynard wrote the autobiographical book Behind the Smiles, which details her life and her message of God bringing triumph through tragedy. She also co-authored Destiny Crossroads: Trusting the Sovereignty of God in Challenging Times.

Religious Leadership: She is recognized as an Apostle within certain religious circles, as noted in a discussion on the Women Empowering Women lifestyle talk show.

Message and Focus: Her work and public presence are centered on her faith, her servant's heart, and her message of hope, encouraging people to see God in the midst of difficult circumstances.

International Reach: Maynard's desire is to travel the world and touch lives, reflecting a global perspective on her spiritual mission.

ABOUT THE BOOK

Behind the Smiles is the riveting life story of Gaylean Maynard, a Bahamian woman of God whose rite-of-passage conveys the message that God will get in the midst of tragedy and causes triumph.

About the Author: Gaylean Maynard, 66, native of the Commonwealth of the Bahamas who is very passionate about encouraging people from all walks of life that no matter what challenges you face, you can overcome them by keeping a positive attitude by keeping a positive attitude.

www.ingramcontent.com/pod-product-compliance
Lightning Source LLC
Chambersburg PA
CBHW050707160426
43194CB00010B/2031